LOVE MADE ME WAIT

LOVE MADE ME WAIT

By Michelle Ellisa Drew

Copyright: © by Michelle Ellisa Drew 2023

All rights reserved. No part of this book shall be reproduced, stored in a retrieval system, or transmitted by any means, electronic, mechanical, photo copying, recording, or otherwise, without written permission from the publisher. No patent liability is assumed with respect to the use of the information contained herein. Although every precaution has been taken in the preparation of this book, the publisher and author assume no responsibility for errors or omissions. Neither is any liability assumed for damages resulting from the use of information contained herein.

Unless otherwise noted, all Scripture is taken from the King James Version of the Bible.

Scripture quotations marked NASB are from the New American Standard Bible. Scripture quotations taken from the New American Standard Bible®, Copyright © 1960, 1962, 1963, 1968, 1971, 1972,1973,1975, 1977, 1995 by The Lockman Foundation Used by permission. (www.Lockman.org)

Scripture quotations marked (NKJV) are taken from the New King James Version ©1979, 1980, 1982, 1984 by ThomasNelson, Inc. Scripture quotations marked (NLT) are taken from the Holy Bible, New Living Translation, copyright ©1996, 2004, 2015 byTyndale House Foundation. Used by permission of Tyndale House Publishers, Carol Stream, Illinois 60188. All rights reserved.

Scripture quotations taken from the Amplified® Bible Classic, Copyright © 1954, 1958, 1962, 1964, 1965, 1987 by TheLockman Foundation Used by permission." (www.Lockman.org) Scripture quotations marked NIV are from the New International Version, copyright © 1973, 1978, 1984, by InternationalBible Society.

ISBN: 979-8-218-32286-1

Printed in the United States of America

Editor: Daphney Chaney

Interior Design: Marvin D. Cloud

For ordering and other information contact: 281-748-4810.

DEDICATION

I dedicate this book to my mother, Carolina "Beverly Ann" Fields. She raised me in a Christian environment, and I know that it is because of her that I am the woman that I am today. Growing up, I watched her unselfishly make sacrifices for her children. As a child, I saw many imitations, but I must say that she was my first, true example of a *Single Christian Woman of Excellence*. She gave me many necessary tools for womanhood.

Proverbs 22:6 says, "Train up a child in the way he should go: and when he is old, he will not depart from it." Most importantly, she trained me in the ways of the Lord and for that I am and will be eternally grateful.

I love you, mommy!

TABLE OF CONTENTS

Introduction	1
Chapter 1. Love	7
Chapter 2. Her Story: For Better or For Worse	15
Chapter 3. Battered, Bruised, and Broken	23
Chapter 4. When God is Silent	33
Chapter 5. Unanswered Prayers are Often Unexplained Miracles	49
Chapter 6. Love Waited on Me	59
Chapter 7. Love Made Me Wait	67
ENDNOTES	79
About the Author	81

INTRODUCTION

There were signs that my marriage was deteriorating. I was warned several times through dreams and prophetic words that we would no longer be together. However, in my mind, the devil was a liar.

I remember about a year and half before we split, one of my dear friends and classmates was in town preaching a revival. I decided to go. We had not seen one another in over 15 years. In the middle of his message, he said to me, "Woman of God, I see everyone who is close to you walking away from you one by one. It is going to devastate your life. But know this, when it happens, it is the Lord." Unbelievably, I received the same exact prophecy more than once.

During that time, I was hosting women's ministry meetings once a month in a hotel. We were a small group. Most of them could have been my daughters, therefore, we were all close. I don't remember exactly what happened and it is not important, but division came and destroyed it.

One by one, they left. Although it hurt, it did not break me. I assumed this was what the man of God meant, but it was only the beginning of something far worse.

The idea of marriage for most of us is that childhood fairy tale. However, anyone who has been married for an extended period of time understands the unpredictability of seasons. Sometimes, it's hot in winter and some days, a cool enough breeze in spring will feel like winter. There were seasons in my marriage when I felt as if I didn't love my husband; I even struggled to like him, but I never left, and I never cheated.

Eventually, things would shift, and I'd learned to love him again. To me, the challenges at hand, were no different. My thoughts remained centered on the past victories. My husband and I had been through a lot and always found our way to overcome obstacles. Overcoming gives us a sense of power. That power creates a force within us that refuses to believe in anything other than the best. Selflessly, I gave my all, and my ex-husband took all I was willing to give. As much as it gave me hope, it also left me depleted.

I've come to realize that life doesn't always happen how we imagine. Rather, life is one carefully written story filled with many chapters. Sometimes, edits will be necessary because of its volumes. Occasionally, it may seem unfinished and could potentially end abruptly. Various characters or people will be removed or torn out of your life just like pages that fall out of a book, but it is still your story.

This book is a part of my story. Writing it gives me freedom and a release from things of my past. I am closing some chapters and opening others. In recent years, I have finally come to realize and appreciate God's reason for the carefully planned journey of my life, and I am now living a small part of what I believe to be my destiny. We are all appointed a span of time to fulfill a purpose. That time or life is filled with a series of events. Generally, we do not choose the order in which we encounter them. The sequence in which things occur is in God's hands, as He is manager and director. I am certain that nothing ever happens by chance, and nothing remains the same. For everything in our lives there is a season.

"To everything there is a season, and a time to every purpose under the heaven: A time to be born, and a time to die; a time to plant, and a time to pluck up that which is planted; A time to kill, and a time to heal; a time to break down, and a time to build up; A time to weep, and a time to laugh; a time to mourn, and a time to dance; A time to cast away stones, and a time to gather stones together; a time to embrace, and a time to refrain from embracing; A time to get, and a time to lose; a time to keep, and a time to cast away; A time to rend, and a time to sew; a time to keep silence, and a time to speak; A time to love, and a time to hate; a time of war, and a time of peace" (Ecclesiastes 3:1-8).

A few years ago, in 2007 to be exact, I was invited to teach at a women's conference. My subject to my surprise was "Love." The Bible is filled with numerous references to God's love, therefore, I had no idea where to begin. I could have chosen a topic myself, but when God gives you a word to teach others, His plan is greater than it appears. That plan often includes a message to the messenger. God designs it so that correction, healing, and deliverance is illuminated. I was not in a good place mentally or emotionally while preparing for the message. I was also separated from my now ex-husband. We were together 17 years before we divorced in March of 2010. I needed God to speak to me personally.

I'm not here to bash him or any man. He had his issues and I had mine; however, the marriage was not all bad. We have three children, and there was a time when we really loved one other, and we were very happy. We had a beautiful home with a pool in the back yard. We enjoyed family vacations every year and we were able to send our youngest son to private school. We appeared to have the "American Dream." By the time the trouble in our marriage began, our two eldest sons, had already moved out. Which left our youngest son exposed to our dysfunction.

I want everyone to know that I'm going to be transparent in this book. I believe healing comes when we are open and honest with ourselves and with others. The world has a 12-step program for those struggling with addiction. The first step is to admit you have a problem. I believe some of those same steps should be followed if we want to be healed and delivered.

First, you must admit you have a problem and how you got there. You don't have to tell me, but you need to tell someone. You must also be honest with yourself and with God. Find a trusted counselor or friend. Be sure it's someone who is committed to sincerely praying for you. As we are told in James 5:16, "Confess your faults one to another, and pray one for another, that ye may be healed. The effectual fervent prayer of a righteous man availeth much."

When I started writing this book, I vowed to myself that I would share intimate moments with you. I am a private person, therefore, revealing my truth, was scary. But I knew God wanted the intricate details of my healing conveyed so that whoever reads this book, would know they are not alone, and God restores.

If you have experienced hurt in any form, don't let anyone tell you to "just get over it" because it's not that simple. Rushing the healing process often forces us into covering pain instead of facing it. One minute, you may feel completely healed, and the next minute, a memory or conversation, can trigger the same pain.

If that happens, it will appear to you and others that you are not healed. Past pain isn't always an indication of unhealed emotions; it's how you deal with the pain that reveals whether you simply survived it or conquered it.

As you turn the following pages, bear with me until the end. I'm sure you will explore a plethora of emotions; if not because I've hit a spot in the depth of your own pain, it will be because you are appalled at the intensity of mine.

Either case, join me and you will be empowered to rise in the fullness of real love. A radical love that will erase any false ideas of what you thought your life should be, into embracing the life that God has predestined. *Love made me wait.*

Chapter One:

Love

I went through some boxes a few weeks ago and I came across one of my old journals. I skimmed through one of them and saw an entry from 2014. It was a prayer about the man I wanted to love me.

Dear God, I want and need a man that is kindhearted and attentive. I want and need a man that is concerned about what I'm feeling. I want and need a man that is gentle, soft spoken, compassionate, and sensitive. I want and need a man that can articulate his love for me and doesn't have issues doing it. I want and need a man that is affectionate and that goes out of his way for me. I want him to make love to me with his eyes and his smile. I never want to question his love. I want to lay on his chest and listen to his heartbeat. I want to look at him from across the room and blush. I want to walk with him in the park and early mornings on the beach. I want to watch reruns of old movies with him. I want to cook him breakfast for dinner. I want to lay next to him and watch him sleep while praying for him. I want him to hold me like he never wants to let go and kiss me like I'm his first.

After reading this, I thought to myself, *Wow!* but, please no judgment. This is what I felt I needed at the time. Before we become mature, our "love" requests are often shallow and surface level. I realized all of it was about what I thought I wanted and needed. Those requests were centered around my definitions of love at that time. As I've matured, I can see there was nothing included about what I was willing to give of myself.

After heartbreak, I was left questioning the definition of love. Did anyone know? We all have our own definition of what we think love is or should be. I found out that there are four different types of love relationships. I want to talk about them for just a moment.

There is Eros. It is the erotic, romantic, sensual, or passionate love. It's more often about the person who is feeling sexual, than it is about the person who is the focus of that love. In other words, this love can be selfish. This is the love between a husband and wife and should be reserved for marriage.

There is also Storge love. This refers to family love. A love that is natural or the instinct of a parent towards their children and vice versa. There is normally no physical contact but is more of a bond or kinship love.

Philia is brotherly love. The love you have for your brothers and sisters in Christ. This is a friendship type of love.

Last, and the most important is Agape love. This love is perfect and pure. It is given even when it is not returned. It is the highest and purest form of love. It loves without motive and without expectation. This is godly love.

Merriam-Webster defines love as an intense feeling of deep affection for someone or something. For some people love can become an addiction. A distorted view of love can cause toxic behaviors like codependency and emotional weakness.

I remember the first time I thought I was in love. The euphoric feeling of love caused butterflies and goosebumps. I could hardly eat or sleep. Just thinking about him caused tears to swell up in my eyes. A moment away from him, felt like an eternity. It was almost as if I needed his air to breathe.

An improper view of love is often mingled with impurities, such as, selfish motives, agendas, deceit, and manipulation. They are often conditional and filled with statements like, "If you love me, you will do this." Or "Because you hurt me, you can't love me." I've even heard some people say, "Love means never having to say you're sorry." Well, we all know that isn't true because we are all born in sin and shaped in iniquity. Man is fallible and at some point, we will fail. Apologies and forgiveness will definitely be needed.

I do believe our definition of love changes as we walk through life. We start to see things differently over time. What we believed to be love when we were younger was actually infatuation. When I look back now, I ask myself, *what was I thinking?* As I mature, love has a totally different meaning. Love means I must make sacrifices. It also means that I grow in patience and remain vulnerable even at the risk of being hurt. Our definitions may vary as everyone gives and receives love differently.

Alford Lord Tennyson said, "It is better to have loved and lost, than to never have loved at all." Lost love is still love. Lost love is painful. It breaks to the core causing the heart to bleed. The emotional toil of a broken heart can take a while to mend. It can cause mental and emotional instability. It is also a breeding ground for unforgiveness, hate, and bitterness. Some of the byproducts of a broken heart are fear, low self-esteem, and addictions. Review the following scriptures on the heart.

Proverbs 12:25 says, "Heaviness in the heart of man maketh it stoop, but a good word maketh it glad." Proverbs 4:23 says, "Keep thy heart with all diligence for out of it are the issues of life." The soul is made up of the mind, will, intellect, and emotions.

Many times, the word heart in the Bible has reference to the soul as in this Scripture. "Therefore, watch your heart [soul] and pay attention to it. Guard and protect what goes into it, what you allow to control it, and what comes out of it." That same verse says, "For out of it, springs the issues of life." The NLT says, "For it determines the course of your life."

When we fail to guard our hearts, we can allow the bitterness of tainted love to govern how we relate to others and how we treat ourselves. Especially when we give our all to a person and love isn't reciprocated. We start to believe we are unloveable and we begin to question our own self-worth.

Love relationships often force us to peer deep within our souls to discover why we react or fail to act in certain situations. My marriage taught me that I depended on the love of my husband for my joy. When there was a deficit in his love towards me, joy dissipated. I realized I'd been controlled by my own need for love. It isn't that heartbreak isn't supposed to hurt us, it should. However, my pain was more about me than him. Finding that truth was not easy. I've discovered it is hard to know real joy if there has never been true sorrow. And it is difficult to appreciate life, if not at some point we've also become acquainted with death.

Joy in the Bible by Greek definition is the word [charas]. It is closely intertwined with the Greek word for grace [charis]. It is in God's grace; unmerited favor that we find true joy. It is the joy of our salvation, and the joy of discovery. I found that I misplaced my joy, because it was in discovering God's love for me that joy began to flourish from my soul once again.

Finding Closure

Like most people, I've longed for closure before moving forward. Waiting on closure, prolongs healing. When we demand others give us the answers for their departure, we are in danger of idolatry. No one is responsible for us resolving to move forward into the future. We don't need permission to heal. We only need surrender. God created us and He is the only one who can complete us. Love relationships can be beautiful, but they were never designed to replace the relationship we have with God. You're probably thinking, *my relationship with God is independent.*

Trust me, I've been there. However, when a heart finally connects to another heart in ways you've only imagined and dreamed about, something happens to these emotionally charged unions.

They ignite the soul with such a fervor, that ripping them apart creates mental and soul confusion. Longing for that love again, can easily develop into interdependence instead.

We must get to a place where we accept what is and move into different possibilities. Moving forward does not mean that grief will be avoidable. To the contrary, grief is a necessary part of life, love, and loss. In healthy love, the transition from former habits and thought patterns can bring a level of grief. Other times, we often grieve what brought us a sense of purpose, even if it was shattered or broken love.

I have also come to understand that before the day of my conception, some things were already predetermined and inevitable. Nothing has happened to me, good or bad, nor will happen that God does not know about. Whether He strategically purposed them or allowed them based on my decisions and choices, He still finds a way to get the glory. I know that sounds religiously cliché, especially depending upon the extent of the bad things.

Nevertheless, during it all, the maturity and wisdom I've gained can aid others in facing the storms in their own lives. Although I have experienced relentless obstacles, and my life appeared as though it has been plagued by devastation, I am assured and confident that all of it is still working for my good.

The issues with my marriage began in 2007 and I am writing this book in 2022. It has been 10 years since my divorce was final. Years later, 15 to be exact, as I am typing this, the thoughts from my past still cause a twinge of pain. Even though I've grown by leaps and bounds, there are certain things that may trigger anxiety within me. I realize that I will live with the scars and memories for a lifetime. But I also believe that scars are sometimes necessary so people can see where you've been. When I think of scars, I'm reminded of the disciple Thomas. After the resurrection, Jesus appeared to the 12, but Thomas could not believe it was Jesus. (John 20:25-29).

This unbelief is where we get the phrase, "doubting Thomas." Jesus had to let Thomas touch His scar before he would believe. Some people won't believe until they see your scars or hear your story. Never be ashamed of them. If you are healed, they will help shape you into a better person. Even if you are still in the process of healing, please know that shame will only rob you of courage. Confront the fear and press on!

Trust me, writing this book pushed me beyond any limitation and barrier I set for myself. Releasing is even harder than I thought. I held this manuscript with a tight grip, afraid of what is written and afraid of what isn't. My release was not void of opposition. Some well-meaning friends didn't think I could do this, but God sends the right people into our lives when we need them the most. The push I needed came. I did it afraid. Fear may be present, but never again, will I allow it to paralyze me.

Withholding this portion of my journey, would also mean withholding breakthrough for my bloodline and yours. I could no longer stand in the way. Love gave me closure.

> **NUGGET:**
>
> *No one is responsible for us resolving to move forward into the future, except US!*

CHAPTER TWO:

HERSTORY; FOR BETTER OR FOR WORSE

I was raised in the small town of Sweeny, Texas. My religious background is COGIC, (Church of God in Christ). Some of the religion's rules centered around women being modest. Modesty in that sense, meant we were forbidden to wear makeup, cut our hair, or wear pants. My mom and dad split up when I was around eleven. My mom tried to make it work, but my dad didn't, and that was that.

Nonetheless, I was still taught if things went wrong in a marriage, to stay, pray, and believe that God would restore it, and from what I witnessed, He usually did. The prayer circle of wives and mothers in the church came together to intercede for wayward husbands.

I remember wives who refused to leave their homes, instead they chose to remain steadfast in believing God for a different outcome. I'm not saying that this was every woman's resolve, however, from my view, those same marriages that were on the brink of divorce somehow survived.

In hindsight, I can see where my vision regarding marriage may have been clouded by those testimonies. My journey was only beginning.

When I attended college, my life wasn't completely mapped out. I got pregnant by my high school sweetheart that first year. I came home for Christmas break, and I didn't go back. We had a son. We eventually married and had a second son. We were young and that marriage didn't last. I didn't know what to do to keep it together, therefore, I made stupid decisions and so did he.

When I got married for the second time, I was much older and more mature. I also had a relationship with God. We attended church every Sunday, therefore, I looked at my vows differently. I meant for better or for worse and was determined to see things through this time. I didn't fight for my first marriage; therefore, I was all in this time.

My second husband had my whole heart. He was an amazing husband, minister of God, and a great provider. There wasn't anything that I asked or needed that he didn't do or provide. But as the saying goes, eventually the honeymoon ends. I started to notice slight changes in his behavior. Years later, our marriage began to shift downward. He showed all the signs of a cheating spouse; He didn't come home after work and often disappeared on weekends.

Although his behavior hurt me, I trusted God to fix it and him. God answered so many prayers and had come through before and I knew He would do the same this time.

One night as I drew my husband's bath water and he got undressed, out of the blue, he told me he was going out of town with his mistress and would be back Sunday.

What did he just say?

Yes, you read it right. He told me he was going out of town with her. I was stunned. It was if someone slapped me, stuck a knife in my chest, and ripped my heart out all at the same time.

But instantly, I heard the voice of God say, "Don't say anything" and I didn't.

That Friday, he went to work and never came back. The next time I saw him was two weeks later when he came home to pick up the rest of his clothes. Don't get me wrong, I knew he was cheating, and he had cheated before, but I never thought he would leave and surely, not like that. It confused me. There were many unanswered questions.

In the midst of a lot of crying, I did what I was taught to do, and that was fast, pray, and believe God. I believed God, fasted, and prayed. And I fasted, prayed, and believed God. God was silent. God stayed silent.

Sometimes, while he was away, I'd call him. I wanted my marriage. And I wanted to find out what went wrong. I wanted us to talk things over. Most times, he'd ignore my calls or hang up on me. Something was strange about his cheating this time. I discerned the difference in his attitude towards me.

One night I called, and she answered. I could hear him talking in the background. She asked him if he wanted to talk to me and I heard him say no. She said and I quote. *Well, I'm going to spare you the dirty words that she used, but you can fill in the blanks.*

She said, "You cannot talk to him today, !@#$%. I'm getting my !@#$% licked."

I'm not stupid. I knew he was having sex with other women. But really? Her statement was distasteful, disrespectful, and derogatory. What reason did she have to be upset with me? I was his wife; she was the other woman. Nonetheless, the emotional torment seemed too much to bear.

Can you imagine? Most of you can't. I realize millions of women have been in my shoes, however, every situation is unique to the individual and everyone processes hurt and pain differently. The emotional turmoil it had on my mind was indescribable. At the time, I couldn't conceive anything beyond my own pain, which left me feeling isolated and alone.

Although I knew my ex-husband was having an affair, giving up on my marriage was still far from my mind. We had too much history and had built so much together. I refused to allow an affair to destroy it, besides, she wasn't worth it. Some of you are saying, "That would have been it for me." Maybe it should have been for me too, but love is not something you turn on and off. It's not something you can easily walk away from. It will also make you put up with things that others won't.

The Other Woman

I'd never seen her, and I was curious. You know how we do sisters; we want to see what he left us for. Therefore, I came up with a plan. I called one of my friends. To protect her privacy, I will call her Lena. She and I met up. We went to his job and waited in the parking lot for him to get off work. We wore baseball caps as disguises. He got on the Park-&-Ride Bus, and we followed it. The other woman picked him up. We followed them home and I finally got a chance to see her from a distance. Additionally, now I knew exactly where he lived. Lena and I laughed about what we did. We called this our "Thelma and Louise" moment.

I never went back because I satisfied my curiosity. I couldn't believe he left our nice home to go live in an apartment with her. I thought, *she must have more money than me.* Surely, that was the only explanation. What other reason would he leave? I know I'm crazy, but back then, I would much rather him cheat than leave home. I told you, fear of being alone will make you put up with crazy stuff.

My days and nights were all running together. I was walking around in a fog. I was a stay-at-home mom. After taking my then 12-year-old son to school and coming back home, I'd pray and literally cry all day. I cried so much I forgot how to laugh. At night, it was difficult to lay alone in the bed we used to share. I slept on the floor in my walk-in closet because I didn't want to sleep alone.

I allowed the enemy to toy with my head. Negative thoughts ran through my mind. I was constantly trying to figure out why he'd choose her over me; over us? He left our child to be with her. *What is wrong with me? Am I not pretty enough? Am I too fat or too skinny? Too black?* I kept wondering, *what did she have that I didn't?*

Eventually, I had the opportunity to see her face to face. I mentioned above, after we followed them I got a glimpse of her from the door, but couldn't clearly see her. Well, this time we met face to face. After he'd been living with her for a year, he asked to come back home and of course, I let him. What was I thinking?

One day she had the nerve to come to my home. She was angry that he was back with his wife and son. She was slightly older than me. She also had a couple of gold teeth. Her braids were long down her back, and almost reached her butt. I examined everything about her, down to her lime green nail polish. And her language was extremely vulgar. She cursed like a sailor. I'm not describing her negatively out of anger or bitterness. Even if she'd been pretty, her attitude made her ugly.

As I recall this incident, I'm laughing as I write. Don't judge me. Because there was a time when I could not laugh, regardless of how she presented herself. When she came to our home, she threw his clothes in the front yard and poured Clorox bleach all over them. I thought, *"Ms. Ghetto Fabulous!"* She of course, was nothing like me and nothing like I imagined. Literally, we were total opposites.

I thought he left for a younger woman, or someone better than I was, but he didn't. I recognized that she was probably acting out because she was also in pain. But again, she was nothing like me. Ladies, I'm telling you this because they don't always leave for something better. Get that out of your mind. I realize now that it wasn't about any of that. I have always been an analytical person; therefore, I was trying to figure out why he left. A part of my personality is to try and understand why people behave the way they do. If things do not make logical sense, it messes with my psyche. I am probably in the wrong profession. Maybe I should go to school to become a psychologist.

I didn't know or even understand this back then, but we can get caught up in things and don't know how to get out. At the time, I believed that is what happened with my ex-husband. He got caught up, and he didn't have the strength to get out. I heard someone say, "Sin will take you further than you want to go, and make you stay longer than you want to stay." Moreover, it will also make you pay more than you want to pay.

Sin will destroy your life. Again, sin will destroy your life and the lives of others who are attached to you. This situation produced pain and insecurities that I didn't know could exist. I struggled inwardly. It's hard to describe or adequately put into words, but I became a prisoner of my own pain. I locked myself in.

I have never expressed to anyone the depth of how miserable I felt until now and obviously, it was not evident to those around me. Apparently, no one had the ability to look at me and see my pain. If they did see, they never addressed it. It reminds me of the woman in the Bible with the spirit of infirmity.

"And he was teaching in one of the synagogues on the sabbath. And, behold, there was a woman which had a spirit of infirmity eighteen years, and was bowed together, and could in no wise lift up herself" (Luke 13:10-11).

Like her, I went to church consistently, yet I was still in a position of brokenness for years. No one saw her and no one saw me. I know it's impossible to recognize insecurities by looking at someone. But Sunday after Sunday and Wednesday after Wednesday; no one noticed what I was struggling with. Like the infirmed woman, even when something is abnormal, it can appear normal by the way we carry it. Because my pain was deeply hidden behind my smile, no one heard my silent cry for help.

They couldn't see the frown in my heart, nor tears in my soul. I consistently questioned if God noticed or if He even cared about what I was going through? I repeatedly asked, "Why this and why me?"

> **NUGGET:**
>
> *Like the infirmed woman in Luke 13, even when something is abnormal, it can appear normal by the way we carry it.*

Chapter Three:

Battered, Bruised, and Broken

The problem in my marriage removed my ability to see my value as a woman. As a teenager, I battled depression and it has continued throughout my life. I have always battled with depression. But this situation made it worse. The pain and mental torment was deeper than any pain I'd ever felt. This hole was deep and dark, and everything was out of my control. I felt like I was drowning and gasping for air because I could never catch my breath. I was swallowed up by pain. Anxiety overtook me, and my thoughts raced. Thinking back on it, still brings me to tears.

I fought every day for my sanity. The mental and emotional battle to stay sane became unbearable. At one point, I gave up trying. I prayed and asked God to let me lose my mind because I wanted to be detached from the pain. I was willing to escape at any cost. Yes, you read that correctly. I prayed and asked God to allow me lose my mind. And it appeared I was doing exactly that. I was on the verge of a nervous breakdown. For those of you who don't know what a breakdown is, it is a period of severe emotional distress, where a person may feel paralyzed and entirely incapable of coping with life's challenges. I was in a deep pit and I didn't have the strength to get out. This place was cold. God even allowed everyone I thought I needed to walk away from me.

I was alone and isolated. But as far back as I can remember, God has always been my protector. He did not allow me to be a statistic. He stayed present from a distance. He was far away, yet close enough to watch and still protect me from myself. He left me to deal with the pain to share this story of not only of survival, but also of life. A lot of people who go through what I did, commit suicide, murder, or both.

I told you I'd be transparent. Some of the readers of this book are acquainted with me. You see me after the pain, in this glory, but you don't know "Her-Story" or my history. The magnitude of the pain and agony is still indescribable. I often try to find the words to articulate some or all of my feelings, but I come up empty. I was broken in pieces and in places I never knew could be broken.

During this, I was also watching my youngest son go into a deep dark place. He was only 12 at the time. He is the only child of his father. He and his father were very close so I never thought that his father would leave him.

The decision my ex-husband made affected me and our son. He didn't think about that. He made a selfish choice. I could see the hurt and confusion in my son's face, but I didn't know what to say to him. Although he needed me, I didn't have the strength to carry the both of us. He was a kid, and he didn't know what was going on and surely didn't understand it. I was in pain, but I also carried the pain for my son. I wanted to fix this for him, but my life had spiraled out of control. I was like a blind man grasping in the dark. I was lost and abandoned by the man I loved and thought loved me. I even felt rejected by the God I knew, loved, and served. The same God I'd watched come through for others, would not respond to me. The God who answered prayers before, now hid His face. Did God turn His back on me?

I knew where my husband was. He made his choice transparently clear. But where was God? Why didn't He come see about me and my son? I'd gotten to the point where it was no longer only about my marriage. It was personal. It was about me. I constantly wondered why God left me. What had I done that was so wrong that He now rejected me?

I asked God, "How am I supposed to minister the Word to others from this place?" The gospel I know is about hope. What kind of hope could I give anyone? My life fell apart and crumbled right before my eyes, and I didn't have the strength to teach. How was I supposed to tell women that God would come through for them, when I hadn't experienced it this time myself? And it seemed that He watched me struggle through this pain with no response. This level of pain made me forget about all the previous times God had come through for me.

I was already dealing with a lot and to top it off, He gave me a message about "love." I thought to myself, *Really God, you love me, but you won't come see about me.* I didn't know it then, but life as I knew it would never be the same. This experience ... this one season altered my life forever.

Sometimes change can be for the better, although it may take time to see it clearly. However, your response to any negative situation will play a big role in your advancement. Take comfort in knowing that no matter what happens, if God's hand is on your life, you will always reach your place of destination. The road you take may not be the best route and there may be detours, but remember there is always a reason.

I don't believe God caused the turmoil in my marriage, but He did allow it to happen. I also believe with God all things are possible. He could have repaired the relationship if He wanted to, but He chose not to. I tell people all the time just because things are possible, doesn't necessarily mean that it's His plan or His will. I wasn't sure if my situation was God's will or not. I do know my ex-husband made a choice. And because of his choice, my journey changed.

As I laid on the floor, God reminded me of His words, "My grace is sufficient for thee: for my strength is made perfect in weakness" (2 Corinthians 12:9). He also led me to the book of John. I read with intention. It took a few days to complete the book of John. I stopped midway in Chapter 11. He told me the message on love would come from this chapter. I wasn't sure how this would fit the theme of love, but I allowed the Spirit of God to guide me.

I don't pretend to be a Bible scholar, but I am a student of the Word. Especially if I'm teaching, I believe I need to study. I know God spoke that chapter, but I wanted to know why. I desperately needed a word from Him and expected this chapter to speak to me. I love the Bible. It is filled with stories, and it is put together strategically and meticulously.

Only God could have inspired mere men to do something that great. There is nothing else written no matter how successful it is or was that can compare to it. This book in the Bible was named after its author, John. As I studied, I realized there are only seven miracles performed by Jesus that are recorded in the book of John. He also tells us there are too many miracles to count. "And there are also many other things which Jesus did, the which, if they should be written, I suppose that even the world itself could not contain the books that should be written. Amen" (John 21:25).

You may be familiar with the story of Lazarus. Even if you are not, I'm sure it will bring you the same enlightenment that it brought me. By the time we get to the story of Lazarus, six of the miracles have already been completed. The miracles recorded are, changing the water to wine (John 2), healing of the nobleman's son (John 4), healing of the man at the pool of Bethesda (John 5), feeding the 5000 (John 6), Jesus' walking on water (John 6), and the miracle of the blind man (John 9).

As I continued reading through this chapter, I saw the power of God working through Scripture. Crowds experienced the manifestation of His glory and His authority as He walked through the earth. Learning more about His miracles gave me hope to believe God for the miraculous in my life and marriage. I saw things in this chapter that I failed to see before.

In chapter 11, the author, John, gives us specific details about Lazarus, Mary, and Martha. He not only gives their names but he even provides us with some background information on each of them. He goes on to tell us they are siblings from Bethany. He makes sure we understand who they are. John is scrupulous in this passage of Scripture. He goes to great lengths to make it clear that we know Mary, Martha, and Lazarus have a connection to each other and with Jesus.

Starting with this chapter and throughout this book, I will give you a more detailed description of each of them. I will talk briefly about their personality and character traits. Hopefully, you will see something you can relate too as well. I'm convinced Jesus is showing us there are people who are not meant to remain in our lives. Some relationships are temporary. Learning this has been a hard lesson for me.

Perhaps you too, have come to realize that each person has a particular role in your life. We must be okay with discerning when their time is up, or when our time in their lives has ended.

We don't see Jesus connecting intimately with a lot of people. Scripture shows us He helped them and moved on. However, we find the main characters in this story, Mary, Martha, and Lazarus, sharing a personal relationship with Jesus. Jesus was also a frequent visitor at their home.

I want to talk about Lazarus first. Read John 11:1-2. "Now a certain man was sick, named Lazarus, of Bethany, the town of Mary and her sister Martha. (It was that Mary which anointed the Lord with ointment, and wiped his feet with her hair, whose brother Lazarus was sick)."

Even though he never speaks in this chapter, everything that takes place is centered around him or his condition. Although Lazarus from Bethany is mentioned in a few other places in the gospels, none give complete details about his life.

The Bible doesn't give us any words or discourses from him. It makes me think, *he may have been a man of few words.* I know people who don't talk much, but their presence and their lives speak loudly.

Our lives are often on display. We may not realize it, but someone, somewhere, is always taking note of our character. One of my former pastors can be quoted as saying it this way: "Sister Michelle, God works both ends at the same time. You are often being student and teacher all at the same time."

Like Lazarus, my ex-husband will never speak in this book, but his actions will reverberate loud enough through me that his life will be a testament to all who will receive it. I thought he had a real a relationship with God. He was a minister at the church we attended, and I know God truly loved him. However, his sin, his choice, his condition, and his behavior during our marriage affected everyone around us, mainly my son and I.

The phrase, "I'm grown" has led many to believe that being an adult gives them the license to do as they please. They do not consider the consequences. Good choices, good consequences. Bad choices, bad consequences. Also, there will be times in your life when people will do negative things and they may not be aware of what they did.

Let's look at the biblical account of Lazarus again. Lazarus is sick and couldn't do anything about his condition. He may have been aware of the stress and the pressure that Mary and Martha experienced, but he couldn't alleviate it. He didn't have the ability to heal himself so he surely could not help them. I wonder about people who make poor choices. What about those who are deliberately causing hurt and pain to others? What about those who lie and try to sabotage others? It may not be a physical illness, but it is an illness. Life has taught me that unacknowledged pain is as damaging as unprocessed pain. My thoughts at the time were that my ex-husband and his mistress knew better than to get entangled in an affair. But did they really know better? I didn't get this back then, however, I realize now that they both had something wrong on the inside of them. That something would cause them to negate the fact he was a married man.

To inflict harm upon an individual and not carry the deep feelings of regret or guilt, is often marked by unhealed trauma in some form. Like Lazarus, their condition could only be healed by Jesus. I'm not making excuses for either of them or their behavior. It took healing and growth for me to see beyond the pain I experienced.

According to Merriam Webster, the definition of sick, refers to any condition that causes, pain, dysfunction, distress, social problems and/or death to a person. Sickness can also cause similar problems for those who encounter the ill person. It can be contagious. Sickness comes in many forms. You can be mentally, physically, emotionally, morally, and even financially sick. They were sick. I have no other way to describe it than to call it what it is. Therefore, without trying to bash my ex-husband, I'd say what he was dealing with was the sickness of sin. In trying to find a resolution in my mind and deal with his soulish issues, I had to focus on the fact that he needed inner healing and deliverance. This by no means implies that sin has never been a part of my life.

He was sick with the lust of his flesh. He was also sick with pride and selfishness. However, unlike Lazarus, he had the ability to get someone to help him. Lazarus was dead, my ex wasn't. At any given moment, he could have called on Jesus for help.

NUGGET:

A sin sick soul can only be healed by Jesus Christ.

CHAPTER FOUR:

WHEN GOD IS SILENT

The Bible says in John 11:3, "So the sisters sent word to Him, saying, 'Lord, behold, he whom You love is sick.'" We have established that the siblings all have a relationship with Jesus. But despite their relationship, this problem arose. The sisters sent word to him about their issue. I'm not sure if it was by letter, by word of mouth, or by prayer. Obviously, they didn't doubt the love Jesus had for Lazarus. They are specific in saying, "he whom *you* love is sick."

When I read this text, I see two sisters who are confident in Jesus' ability to restore. Journeying back to Bethany to see about them, was also another indication of His love for them. In the passage, when Martha sees Jesus afar off, she runs ahead to greet Him. She admits she was disturbed that it took four days for Him to come. However, she spoke confidently that even then, God would grant whatever He asks.

I'm going to mess with some of your theology right now. The modern-day church has taught us to think that problems should not exist because Jesus loves us. The fact that she says to Jesus, "If you would have been here, my brother would not have died," tells us her expectations. Being in a relationship with Jesus meant she should not experience pain, especially to that magnitude. I can be the first to admit that I never would have thought that some of the pain in my life would torment me to the extent it has.

Although it is a common consensus that we shouldn't have pain, it is not biblical truth. Jesus paid the price for our salvation. He did not pay the price for life to be free from problems or suffering. If you are saved and have a relationship with God, there is, however a peace that comes along with your salvation. It is the peace that comforts you in dark times of knowing you are not alone. But nowhere in Scripture will you find that your life should or will be immune from problems. Inserted below are some of my favorite Scriptures of encouragement, concerning suffering.

"Many are the afflictions of the righteous; but the Lord delivereth him out of them all" (Psalm 34:19).

"It is good for me that I have been afflicted; that I might learn thy statutes" (Psalm 119:71).

"Yea, and all that will live godly in Christ Jesus shall suffer persecution" (2 Timothy 3:12).

Please note: Life may very well afford you the opportunity to experience pain. The Bible says if you follow the path of righteousness, it is nearly inevitable that you will be persecuted. We are also assured that Jesus will deliver us from all our afflictions. (John 16:33)

I firmly believe that the misunderstandings concerning suffering for a Christian is due to the lack of personal Bible study. Unfortunately, we hear a lot of clichés, and untruth from those who profess Christianity but have no idea what the Bible really says. Relying on others to do your studying of the Bible, will lead to deception. We need Bible teachers; however, we must be diligent in gaining insight for ourselves. This will deepen our relationship with God; therefore, I would encourage you to study the Word for yourself. 2 Timothy 2:15 says to study to show ourselves approved unto God, a workman that needeth not to be ashamed, rightly dividing the word of truth. (Paraphrased)

Seeing myself in the pain of Mary and Martha

The Bible doesn't tell us what kind of illness Lazarus had or how long he had been sick. I did research and the most I could come up with was he had some type of fever or flu. And regardless of his ongoing relationship with Jesus, this sickness proved fatal for Lazarus, so why didn't Jesus come when they sent word to Him?

Furthermore, I wanted to know why didn't God answer me? Many questions plagued my mind. The deep anguish in my soul, caused me to question the authenticity of my relationship with Jesus. I wondered if I'd angered God, or if He had punished me for something. Although I compare our stories, I discovered we were vastly different. Like Mary and Martha, I was sure Jesus would come through for me, too. However, our outcomes were different.

Let us take a deeper look at some background information on the siblings. I love how the author details their distinct personalities. Mary, according to Scripture, is a worshipper. John makes sure his details of her are precise, so that we do not get her confused with Mary Magdalene. He gives a brief illustration of her as one that cries so much in worship that she wipes the feet of Jesus with her hair. However, this act of pure worship does not happen until John 12:3.

Martha on the other hand, who is bold and direct, has a strong personality. She comes across as being strong-willed, forceful, and domineering. But she has the gift of hospitality and service. She is a helper, which causes her to lose focus. Read Luke 10:38-42.

"Now it came to pass, as they went, that he entered into a certain village: and a certain woman named Martha received him into her house. And she had a sister called Mary, which also sat at Jesus' feet, and heard his word. But Martha was cumbered about much serving, and came to him, and said, Lord, dost thou not care that my sister hath left me to serve alone? bid her therefore that she help me."

Don't get me wrong, Martha was doing a good thing. Martha's expectation was that Mary would do the same thing. I would even say she may have resented Mary because she spent a lot of time in worship. She even tells Jesus to ask Mary to help her. We all have gifts. But we don't all have the same gifts.

Let's continue reading, starting at verse 41. "And Jesus answered and said unto her, Martha, Martha, thou art careful and troubled about many things: But one thing is needful: and Mary hath chosen that good part, which shall not be taken away from her."

Both served Jesus. Just in different capacities. Martha possessed the gift of hospitality, while Mary's heart was intent upon worship through listening at His feet. I shared this part about them, because even though we may be serving, worshiping, and praying, our lives can still be interrupted by pain.

When their brother died, the grief must have been unbearable. I can imagine their anger at first, knowing that Jesus delayed in coming. Although we have faith in Jesus, it can be a real mind battle when answers do not come immediately.

Grief happens in many stages for any type of loss. I most certainly grieved my marriage. I was in mourning for a long time. One comforting thought, however, is at least Mary and Martha had one another. My process, like many of yours, left me feeling empty and alone. I had no one to lean on and the situation with my husband got the best of me.

Like the sisters in this biblical story, I too had a relationship with Jesus. I had a specific place and time of day to meet Him. The time has always been early mornings for me to have quiet time with God.

I am familiar with the distress and the emotional roller coaster that Mary and Martha were on. Four days to them seemed like an eternity. I can imagine the anxiety of trying to hold on and believe with every fiber of their being that each day was the day Jesus would show up. I, like many of you, also identify with their pain.

Even though I'm saved, despite my relationship with God, even though I have a prayer life, although I fast, and I read and study my word, my husband betrayed my trust and broke our vows.

Read this excerpt from my journal:

Why would God do this or allow this now? My son is in pain. Where are you God? My marriage is in trouble. Where are you God? This can't be the plan of God for my life. I am still trying to pull it together, because I have to teach this message. We all get excited when good things happen, and we are quick to say it is the will of God. What happens when I call Him, and He doesn't answer? This can't be the will of God. Or is it?

I prayed and reminded God of His Word. I spoke the Word over my situation. I read the following Scriptures aloud. "Call unto me, and I will answer thee, and shew thee great and mighty things, which though knowest not (Jeremiah 33:3). "The righteous cry, and the Lord heareth, and delivereth them out of all their troubles" (Psalm 34:17). "For I know the thoughts that I think toward you, saith the Lord, thoughts of peace, and not evil, to give you an expected end. Then shall ye call upon me, and I will hearken unto you" (Jeremiah 29:11-12). But God was still silent....

When my husband left, I lost track of time. I was emotionally distraught, and I cannot lie, I had a serious problem with God. Most of you would never admit that. But I told you, I would be real, raw, and uncut.

I believe the reason I have the relationship with God I do, is because I have never tried to hide what I have done or how I feel, no matter what happened. Anger, hurt, bitterness, frustration, vengefulness, and even guilt, I've laid it all bare before God.

I mentioned in a previous chapter, to get healed, you need to be honest about where you are. I have always questioned Him about why He was doing things in my life, a certain way. I readily express my frustrations regarding different situations that He allows to transpire. I have even told Him that I've often felt it was unfair. But for some reason, the weight of this trial felt completely different. His silence made it worse.

My days and nights seemed to run together. The length of time my husband was gone went from days to weeks. My emotions were all over the place. I felt my God, the God I know, the One I have relationship with, did not come. Despite my crying, He did not come.

John describes Jesus not only as the Walking Word, but the Living Word. He is full of grace and truth. The same Jesus I sent word to, was healing all manner of sickness and disease. The same Lord the Bible says is All-Seeing and All-Knowing had to know what I was going through. Yet, thoughts consistently plagued my mind, such as, does He know what I'm feeling? Does He see or even care about my situation? I felt as if, the Lord of Host, the Lord strong and mighty and mighty in battle did not show up to fight for me. The word of God says, "For I know the thoughts that I think toward you, saith the Lord, thoughts of peace, and not of evil, to give you an expected end" (Jeremiah 29:11).

That Scripture says when He thinks about me, or when I come across His mind, it is for good and not evil. I am honestly baring my soul to every reader right now, and it does not feel good. As much as I knew about God, the pain made me doubt Him. The same God that told me to call Him and He would answer me and show me great and mighty things, was speaking, but somehow beneath the rubbish in my heart, I could not hear Him. Instead, it seemed as if I called and I cried, but He ignored me and sent me to voicemail. Why did the God I know, suddenly hide His face from me?

The Bible says, but when Jesus got the word that Lazarus was sick, He said, "This sickness is not to end in death, but for the glory of God, so that the Son of God may be glorified by it." For those of you who think that sickness is from the devil, that's not absolute. I know we often reference the story about Job and his illness. But remember, even in that, God removed the hedge from Job and gave Satan access. Some things, God allows so He can let you see yourself, get the glory, and bless you with more later. Some things were orchestrated so that God would be glorified. But that's another story, literally.

We read, "Now, Jesus loved Martha, Mary and Lazarus." However, despite His love for them, the Scriptures say when He heard there was a problem, He stayed where He waited another two days. This doesn't make sense to me. Why didn't He send word to the sisters? What happens when you have a relationship with God, and He says He loves you, but He doesn't respond? There I was again questioning my relationship with God. In the silence of God, faith must go to another level. I was so broken that I could not muster up the faith to see clearly. I judged my situation by the blessings of others. Yes, that comparison trap! The problem with comparison is when coveting is present, we never find the place of gratitude. Because I didn't understand the severity of my pain, I often compared my life to others. I compared my mistakes and sins to those of others that "appeared" worse than mine, yet they seemed happy, blessed, and prosperous. I felt something was terribly wrong with that picture. I now know that pride made me feel as if I deserved better.

It was like the tax collector and the Pharisee in Luke 18:9-14. The Pharisee stood to pray and instead of admitting his own faults and praising God, he exalted himself. He said, "I am not like other men–robbers, evil-doers and adulterers." He also spoke of all the religious things he did, like tithing and fasting. This prayer was filled with pride and lacked humility. Unlike the tax collector, he bowed his head, and admitted his need before God. He acknowledged his own frailty and sin.

Jesus made it known, the tax collector's prayer pleased Him. This showed me how important the heart's posture and attitude is to God. But at the time, my heart was blinded by my own pride.

As I continued to compare my life to Mary and Martha, I felt their anxiety. I'm sure when they sent the word to Him that Lazarus was sick, they expected an immediate response. It's easy for me to imagine Martha, constantly going to check in his room to see if he'd gotten up out of the bed completely healed. Her faith was just that. But I also can feel the disappointment, each time she entered his room to discover him still laying there deathly ill. That is how I felt.

Each time, I came out of prayer with an expectancy, I too was met with disappointment. This was marriage, we did it right. Isn't it supposed to work? I could not conceive that God would allow my husband to walk away from his commitment. How could he make the decision to reject his responsibility to me, our son, and to God?

While they waited for a response from Jesus, Lazarus died. I felt their immense pain, because while I waited, my marriage continued to decay. I couldn't help but feel anger towards God. I had a real problem with Him. I watched as He blessed others. He had the nerve to heal other people's marriages, while mine was falling apart! I was even thinking, "Jesus, even if you don't come, at least send a word!" I was in a true state of desperation. But everything around me was silent.

Why isn't God responding to my call?

In the natural, you know how it is when you call somebody, and they say they are going to call you back and they don't. Or maybe they don't respond at all. That was my agitation. My expectation of God was the same. I heard someone say we are so accustomed to dealing with humans that we begin to treat God like one of them. I know I did. I expected Him to move or at least respond. There is no doubt that Jesus loved Lazarus, Mary, and Martha. The Bible says they knew it too. But regardless of their relationship He doesn't respond the way they want Him to. I cried, prayed, and turned over my plate. I fasted for seven days, with no food, just water. I prayed three times a day and shut off my cell phone. I needed to hear from God. But nothing. Exasperated, I compared God to my ex-husband.

I said to God, "He left and now so have you. I always thought you would be here. But I guess you don't love me either."

No response....

No answer....

Can you see God sitting there, allowing me to pout, vent my frustrations, kick and scream? He wasn't moved by any of it. He knew after all this, His daughter would bounce back. But He would let me discover it the hard way.

It reminded me of the Scripture in the book of Job 23:8-9. "Behold, I go forward, but he is not there; and backward, but I cannot perceive him: On the left hand, where he doth work, but I cannot behold him: he hideth himself on the right hand, that I cannot see him."

The pain and bitterness coupled with what I believed was God abandoning me, opened the door to the enemy. And the enemy caused me to question everything I knew about God. He literally wanted me convinced that God did not love me. And if you are not careful, he will use pain and bitterness to do the same with you.

Read this except from my journal.

> *It was as if he was deliberately hiding from me. Why? Why didn't he respond to my prayer? Why didn't he respond to my cry and my pain? Why is he not responding to my hurt? His response to me at this point is obviously,* NOT TO RESPOND.
>
> *At least with Mary and Martha, they have a word, "This is for the glory of God." But I have nothing. This storm in my life has come through and ripped up everything in its path. Nothing is solid anymore. Everywhere I look is devastation. I can't see how I can recover from this. I am doing my best to keep it together.*

At this point, I hadn't told anyone in our circle, not even my family that Mr. Drew left me, because I still hoped he would come back. I was so lost. I was also embarrassed and ashamed. Days turned to weeks and weeks turned to months and then a year. Yes, you read that right! An entire year passed, and I still wanted my marriage. The tears finally stopped about six months in. Hurt graduated to anger.

Eventually, it progressed to bitterness. Bitterness is dangerous territory. My heart was no longer pure towards God. He also became the object of my pain. I did everything I knew to do, including holding on to the Word, declaring, fasting, and praying, and I still felt abandoned by God.

He didn't even send a word (prophetically) that He cared about what I was going through. At that point in my life, I was highly offended that He would treat me that way. This is another transparent moment. Most of you may be shocked that I've been vocal about my anger towards God. Know that God appreciates honesty. He knows the inner workings of our hearts. Therefore, silent frustration and masked anger is still knowable to the All-Knowing One.

This my story and my moment of truth. Pain, can make you react in ways you never thought possible. This is a reason people must be taught the proper way to process it. I still believe, even with the right methods and best laid plans, enough pain can cause one to miss the mark. But at least, there will be a blueprint. To top it off, God was still silent. The silence of God tests your faith in unimaginable ways. I now know, it's about perspective; God is always speaking, but from where I sat, I needed clear and precise answers. I am this bottom-line kind of straight to the point person. I wrestled for a long time with God because I wanted to understand. We were taught in school that the shortest distance between two points is a straight line. We don't need all that other stuff. It's black or white for me.

As I delve deeper into the life of Mary and Martha, I'm engrossed in their pain, like I'm the missing sister from this story. Literally, we are all feeling some type of way. I know it seems repetitive, however, that is exactly what I was doing. I allowed the enemy to toy with my mind to such an extent that I kept repeating the same phrases and questions. "You say you love me, but you don't come see about me. You say you love me, but you allowed my husband to leave. I prayed about it, but you didn't answer me." This test and trial felt like an indictment against me. I wondered what did I do that was so bad? Read John 11:11-15:

> "This He said, and after that He said to them, 'Our friend Lazarus has fallen asleep; but I go, so that I may awaken him out of sleep.' The disciples then said to Him, 'Lord, if he has fallen asleep, he will recover.' Now Jesus had spoken of his death, but they thought that He was speaking of literal sleep. So Jesus then said to them plainly, 'Lazarus is dead, and I am glad for your sakes that I was not there, so that you may believe; but let us go to him.'"

The situation for Mary and Martha went from bad to worse. By the time Jesus arrived, Lazarus was dead four days. There are times God will allow things to go from bad to worse. In the worse state, some situations will seem as if they are completely over or unrepairable. Lazarus is dead and Mary and Martha have not heard from Jesus. He tells the disciples He is glad He wasn't there so that they might believe. And He says Lazarus is not dead but sleep.

This story is powerful, not only because of the miracles, but because of the lessons in waiting. Even though God speaks in His Word, and throughout creation, we long to hear Him in a more personal way. The Bible tells us that God spoke to Elijah in a still soft voice. When we are pressed, the softness of His voice can get stifled.

Trusting God, when like Job, we can't trace Him, eventually strengthens us and purifies our faith. Looking with my natural eyes, caused me to miss God's direction during this trial. I've learned that there is a difference between my eyes and His. What I see with my natural eyes, is vastly different from what He sees in the spirit.

Jesus said He allowed tragedy in Mary and Martha's life so the disciples might believe. On top of that, He said He was glad He wasn't there. Prior to that in John 11:4; He said, "the sickness is not unto death, but for the glory of God, that the Son of God might be glorified thereby."

As I studied this, I was completely awed by God. If the sisters had heard the things Jesus said to the disciples, they probably would have asked, "What does the disciples believing have to do with our prayer request?" I was also asking myself, *how could God be glorified if my marriage is destroyed? What good can come out of this? Wouldn't it be better if the marriage were repaired?*

Why would God allow this and then tell me, it's for His glory? God's ways are not like our ways; nor are His thoughts like our thoughts.

I was totally bewildered. His plans are always greater than our immediate satisfaction. When we see God for who He is and not who the world sees, our mistakes, or pain tells us that He is, we are best able to navigate this journey in faith.

NUGGET:

When God seems silent, our faith and trust develops the most.

Chapter Five:

Unanswered Prayers are Often Unexplained Miracles

The Bible says Mary and Martha received word that Jesus was on His way. I know the sisters were basket cases full of all kinds of emotions. I was, too.

I told you earlier that Martha was the mouthy one. She had that kind of in-your-face personality. She had no problem confronting anyone. She's not rude, just the no-nonsense type. When she heard that Jesus was coming; she didn't give him an opportunity to get to the house. She went to meet him halfway. Remember, she is hurt, she is grieving, and she feels abandoned. She has heard that Jesus had been healing others because the Bible says his fame went out because of the miracles He performed. She was disappointed that He didn't answer when she needed him too, but she was anxious for a miracle.

Oftentimes we look or judge someone's attitude by their approach. We never consider where that person is mentally or emotionally. Read John 11:21-27.

"Then Martha said to Jesus, 'Lord, if You had been here, my brother would not have died. Even now I know that whatever You ask of God, God will give to You.' Jesus told her, 'Your brother will rise [from the dead].' Martha replied, 'I know that he will rise [from the dead] in the resurrection on the last day.' Jesus said to her, 'I am the Resurrection and the Life. Whoever believes in (adheres to, trusts in, relies on) Me [as Savior] will live even if he dies; and everyone who lives and believes in Me [as Savior] will never die. Do you believe this?' She said to Him, 'Yes, Lord; I have believed and continue to believe that You are the Christ (the Messiah, the Anointed), the Son of God, He who was [destined and promised] to come into the world [and it is for You that the world has waited].'" AMP

Martha doesn't understand and says I know he will rise at the resurrection. Even though Martha has a relationship with Jesus, she failed to grasp the full meaning of His words. We can miss the true essence of what God intends to show us if we cling to religious mindsets and what we've been taught. We may recognize a level of God's power but lack the wisdom to understand the deeper things of God.

Martha makes the resurrection the object of her faith. But that thought seemed too far away, therefore, she bid Him to ask the Father, for a right now miracle. Thus, her pleading, "Even now, God will do whatever you ask." She knew Jesus the Miracle Worker, was backed by the power of God.

Mary at the urging of her sister, finally pulls herself up from weeping, and goes out to meet Jesus. Reading the next few verses of Scripture, we can sense her tone.

Grief and sorrow had overtaken her. She too was offended by Jesus' delay. Even though she had an attitude, Jesus ignored it. I love this because I see these sisters, naturally and spiritually. Jesus dealt with them where they were in their relationship with Him. Even though they were experiencing the same crisis, He didn't deal with them in the same manner.

Too often, because we have had a similar experience, we want others to respond the way we did. STOP. Stop trying to make people act like, dress like, be like and respond to God the way you do. If He receives them, allow them to develop their own relationship with God. It is your job to plant a seed and water it. You are not responsible for making it grow. Jesus loved Mary and Martha, but He didn't give them what they wanted when they thought they should have it.

Now faith is the substance of things hoped for, the evidence of things not seen. **(Hebrews 11:1)**

God doesn't always respond when we think He should. He does that for good reason. He is trying to teach us to trust Him even though we can't see or understand what He is doing. Tests come to try and develop our faith. When we fail His test, He gives retakes in the same areas. Trust me. I know. As the saying goes, "I've been there and done that and I have my own T-shirt."

While I was preparing to teach on the topic of love; I was right where these siblings were. I was still striving to grow in a lot of areas, primarily my faith. Suddenly, it hit me! Jesus showed up for Mary, Martha, and Lazarus, but not for me. As enlightening as the eleventh chapter of John had been for me, I could not shake the thought that my outcome wasn't the same. There was no resurrection of my marriage. My husband had not come forth out of his grave clothes.

This entire situation with Mary, Martha and the sickness, death and resurrection of Lazarus plays out in Scripture in 44 verses, four days, 96 hours, and 5760 minutes. He didn't show up when they asked him to, but at least He came. By now, you are probably saying, "Girl, get over it already!" That's the problem with us; we always want to hurry another person's process. We can't. God must deal with everyone in the time He orchestrates. Offense heals in time, but it depends on the gravity of the offense. Allow people room to heal. If you are not capable of dealing with people where they are, please leave them to a professional therapist. Your interference could be more of a hindrance, than help.

The situation with my husband was a culminating series of life events that led to extreme rejection. Things I had yet to confront from my past, resurfaced in how I handled our marital issues. This situation left a hole on the inside of me. I felt empty and dry. The foundation of a desert without water will eventually crack. That was me. My well had run dry. I was deeply fractured.

Paralyzed by the pain, I felt trapped in a moment in time. It was like watching one of those old movies about time travel and instead of coming back to the present, the person gets stuck in that era. As difficult as it is to believe, I felt completely rejected and abandoned by God. My relationship with Him seemed dead, like my marriage. When my marriage fell apart, a part of me died, therefore, I saw myself as a type of Lazarus. I wasn't living; I was existing. I was sick with hurt, and it turned into unforgiveness towards my husband and the other woman.

However, Jesus called Lazarus forth. While I was thinking that my husband needed to come forth, I finally had an epiphany! I realized it was me who needed to shake the grave clothes. I hear you saying, "It's about time!" But wait, it doesn't end there.

Before I give you the details of my deliverance in the final chapters of this book, I want to share how dangerous idolatry is. It is difficult to believe that a heart that longs to be loved and cherished can become involved in idolatry, but it's true. The idea of love and marriage distorted my perception.

After a year of being gone, my husband asked to come back home. I allowed it, although he was still cheating with his mistress. I lowered my standards so much that I would have done anything to have "us" again. I was willing to share him as long as I could have a part of him. Is your mouth is hanging open? There's an old song by Betty Wright, *No Pain, No Gain*. In it she says, "Having a piece of man, is better than having no man at all."

Unfortunately, many of us ascribe to that kind of idealogy. Unhealed wounds create a hole that we try to fit everything into, even if we do it by force. The pursuit of personal completeness is often stopped at eros [romantic love]. After all, isn't that what songs and movies portray?

They show us that completeness comes when two people align and God writes their masterpiece of a love story.

Romantic love is beautiful, but when it becomes the source of fulfillment, it is a false god. Well, I need not detail what happened when he returned home. Just know it didn't work. It couldn't work. Relationships that are on the throne in our lives, essentially, receive the worship that belongs solely to God. Relationships turned idolatrous, will never satisfy. Thus, they lead to more disappointment, pain, and bitterness.

Let's return to Mary, Martha, and Lazarus for a moment. Even though Jesus showed up for Mary and Martha, Lazarus was buried and the Bible says "his body stinks." Jesus said, "Did I not say to you that if you believe [in Me], you will see the glory of God [the expression of His excellence]?" (AMP)

I had to know why the part about him with a foul order was mentioned. So of course, I did an investigation. When I researched the word *stink*, it means to be offensive.

We get to the climax in this story in the next few verses. Martha tells Jesus that her brother has been dead 4 days and mentions the decaying of his body has produced a foul order. God doesn't leave anything to chance. These things were spoken and recorded that we know Lazarus isn't asleep or pretending. The miraculous resurrection has called forth new life. There was no mistaken identity, or fabrication, just the pure miracle of resurrected life. Martha's words about the decaying stench, indicated that the woman who said, "even now, I know God will do whatever you ask," came to a point of doubt. To her, his decayed body meant it was too late. But Jesus knowing her doubt, responded, "Did I not tell you, that if you believed, you would see the Glory of God?"

I saw myself in each character in this narrative. Just as you may see yourself in anyone of us, if not all. Some of you are in situations right now that have left you offended and bitter. Some may be filled with doubt or unbelief. Just as Martha, the length of time it takes to see the hand of God displayed, can make you think it's too late. God allowed the news of Lazarus death to spread, so that there could be a great cloud of witnesses to his resurrection.

Unanswered prayers don't always mean God's answer is "No." Sometimes, it is simply "Not yet." His non-response was a set up for a miracle.

I finally reached a point, where the thought of myself decaying inside, made me sick. I'd been in this state far too long, and I wanted the pain to stop. It was time for the emotional roller coaster to end.

Jesus showed up for me, but it wasn't in the way I expected. No, He didn't come to restore my marriage. He came to restore my heart. I hadn't realized how deeply my heart had become hardened. I built huge walls to prevent anyone from hurting me again. Those walls also prevented me from seeing God's hand orchestrating my life.

I'd finally come to the point of decision. I had to be intentional about my own healing and deliverance. It started with repentance for the sin of doubt and unbelief. Next, I repented for the sin of unforgiveness. Once those chains fell off, my heart became pliable enough for God to shape and mold. It wasn't an overnight process.

What are you feeling as you read this? Are you tormented by demons of your past experiences or choices? We may not have the same issue. For instance, yours could be a cheating or abusive spouse, a wayward child, a strife causing relative, church hurt, etc. Maybe it isn't anyone else at all, perhaps you are facing the consequences of your own choices and decisions. Whatever the situation is, God can fix it. He has the answers, even if it isn't the answers you expect.

Jesus asks, "Where have ye laid him?" They said unto Him, "Lord, come and see." I love this because when He asked, it wasn't because He didn't know. Through this text, I can hear Jesus asking you, the reader of this book, where are you buried? Only you know how you got to the place, grave, or tomb you are in. Are you having flashbacks? Are you seeing yourself? Maybe your mind is going back to the times when you've prayed or called Jesus, and He delayed in responding. Where have you buried your pain? Like me, have you piled pain on top of pain? Have you buried your hope or your faith in God because you didn't think He would come? Time may be far spent, and some of you might have given up on praying, asking, and believing.

I had to write this book so you could be healed. Go back to that place where you were wounded or disappointed. Re-visit if you must, the place where you failed and now you are consumed by condemnation, shame, or guilt.

The Bible says, Jesus wept. He cried because everyone stopped believing. Even when he showed up, they still didn't believe. Believe that He is wherever you are. He sees and He cares. Read the final part of this Bible story.

"Jesus wept. Then said the Jews, Behold how he loved him! And some of them said, Could not this man, which opened the eyes of the blind, have caused that even this man should not have died? Jesus therefore again groaning in himself cometh to the grave. It was a cave, and a stone lay upon it. Jesus said, Take ye away the stone. Martha, the sister of him that was dead, saith unto him, Lord, by this time he stinketh: for he hath been dead four days. Jesus saith unto her, Said I not unto thee, that, if thou wouldest believe, thou shouldest see the glory of God? Then they took away the stone from the place where the dead was laid. And Jesus lifted up his eyes, and said, Father, I thank thee that thou hast heard me. And I knew that thou hearest me always: but because of the people which stand by I said it, that they may believe that thou hast sent me. And when he thus had spoken, he cried with a loud voice, Lazarus, come forth. And he that was dead came forth, bound hand and foot with graveclothes: and his face was bound about with a napkin. Jesus saith unto them, Loose him, and let him go. Then many of the Jews which came to Mary, and had seen the things which Jesus did, believed on him" (John 11:35-45).

Jesus could have resurrected Lazarus without them removing the stone. Remember, He is God in the flesh. But there are times when you must play a part in your own deliverance. Jesus is so strategic that He has the men move the stone, then calls Lazarus forward. Lazarus could have sat there sulking that he was allowed to get sick and die, but instead, he walked into his miraculous healing. He wasn't just resurrected, even though that's powerful; every organ in his body had shut down and his flesh started to decay. Jesus healed his entire being.

NUGGET:

God's silence doesn't mean God's absence.

CHAPTER SIX:

LOVE WAITED ON ME

Lazarus' death and resurrection gave witness to the power of Jesus Christ, as a result, many believed. Even though he never says a word verbally, his testimony still speaks. The Scripture says, "Then many of the Jews which came to Mary, and had seen the things which Jesus did, believed on him" (John 11:45).

I'm sure Lazarus would have chosen another way to witness or to glorify God. But God sometimes takes things out of our control so He can get the glory. I find it amazing that a crowd gathered at the tomb of Lazarus. Did they anticipate a miracle? Where they simply being nosey? Scripture tells us that many witnessed it and left to report it to the Pharisees. This prompted a meeting of the Sanhedrin counsel.

As astonishing as the miraculous resurrection of Lazarus was, the Pharisees still found cause for criticism. They thought the people would begin to follow Jesus and no longer listen to them. Their jealousy caused the High Priest to prophecy that Jesus would die for the whole nation. (Verses 46-53) It was the catalyst for the crucifixion. There was a much higher plan at work.

The crowd gathering made me think of how there is always someone watching your life. Many times, God will use you as the sacrifice to die to self, so that life can spring forth. John 12:24 says, "I tell you the truth, unless a kernel of wheat is planted in the soil and dies, it remains alone. But its death will produce many new kernels—a plentiful harvest of new lives."

At times, you may be the one hurt, for others to understand God's healing. I know you don't like it, but it's true even if you do not understand it. Lazarus death and resurrection produced renewed life for him, all of those who witnessed the miracle, and eventually, the entire world was saved through Jesus Christ. Our lives are to be a testament or testimony that Jesus Christ is Lord.

Along our journeys the roads and directions we take differ from each other. God strategically and carefully orchestrates our paths. Even when it appears we've veered off the right road, when we look back, we can see the hand of God. I finally realized my lenses were blurry. I allowed all the junk in my past, and the failure of my marriage to cloud my view. My eyes betrayed me, because only seeing it as divorce, created too much pain.

When the divorce was over, I continued to face mental and emotional shame. I felt like I had been stripped naked and publicly violated. It was humiliating to face gossip, false accusation, and ill-treatment. Some people even made me feel as if the turn of events were all my fault. It was emotionally draining, and I never thought I would recover. Finally, concluding that my ex-husband didn't divorce me, but God delivered me, was liberating! Through one moment, (one bad decision made by someone else) my entire life shifted. All I'd known for 20 years crumbled under the weight of lust and sin. I went from being married to being divorced; from having a "complete" household to navigating life as a single parent; from Mrs. to Ms. The pain took a toll on my mind, body, and spirit, however, as I surrendered to God, I understood the ending is also a beginning.

Instead of only focusing on my ex-husband, my relationship with God grew deeper. With each level, layers of my heart were repaired. I learned and unlearned. I call it "Life lessons 101." The chapters are still being written, but at least I can now face them with hope.

The Bible teaches us that we go from death unto life. It also teaches us that Jesus came that we might have life and have it more abundantly. Until I died to self, I couldn't live unto *Christ*. Dying to self meant I had to let go of what I thought made me whole, and embrace the God who is whole. In Him, we have everything we need. Even if you are walking and breathing, you are only existing if you haven't found life in Christ.

My deeper connection to God was not an overnight process. I still had wounds, and they caused me to close myself off from people. I talked to them and even hung out for a minute, but there was always a wall between us. That wall closed me in and kept everything and everybody else out. It was a safe place, so I thought. I made up my mind that no one would ever hurt me like that again. And I meant no one.

One day I was in my living room watching TV and out of the blue, the Lord began to talk to me. Yes, God does still talk. But most of the time, we don't listen. There was a bookshelf next to the TV and the Lord said, "Look up." When I looked, in the spirit, there was a box on top of the bookshelf with a padlock on it.

I asked him, "What is that?"

He said, "You've put your heart in that box. I want to heal you, but I can't get to it. I need you to take down the box, open it and give me your heart." And immediately, I broke down.

What did God just ask me to do? I thought to myself, "*I can't.*"

Let's go back a moment. All of this with my husband started in 2007 and we officially divorced in March 2010. It was now 2014. I endured seven years of emotional torment. Seven is also the Biblical number of completion, fulfillment, and perfection. 1 Peter 5:10 tells us, after we have suffered a little while that God would perfect, strengthen, and establish us. It doesn't have to take seven years for healing, but in my case it did.

My life went though many transitions. At the time of the divorce, I had been a stay-at-home mom for the last three years. My son went to a Christian private school for several years. After the divorce, I couldn't afford the tuition and he was forced to attend public school. I also lost my house and my car. Eventually, I was left homeless with a teenaged son. You do know that if you don't have your own address, you are still considered homeless, even if you are living with your mother. This was difficult for me. I'd always been able to pull it together and make it, but this time I didn't have the strength. Every part of my life was destroyed.

Suddenly, hearing from God, made me angrier! Why now? How could He show up after all of this and tell me He wants to heal me? In that moment, I was once again flooded with a plethora of emotions. All the bitterness and pain rushed back into my mind. I sobbed uncontrollably. Again, I begin to question, *why did it have to happen in the first place? Couldn't all of it have been prevented?* I screamed, "God you had the power to fix it! Why didn't you?" There I was back in the same place.

There is nothing like a therapy session to force you to face the pain you desperately try to conceal. My therapy wasn't with a licensed professional therapist. I had a one on one with God. Reliving the pain was as tormenting as it was when it first happened. Opening my heart to God, also meant I had to be vulnerable enough to also open it to others and I wasn't ready.

I've taken you on an emotional ride with me. And by now, you're probably ready to get to the end of the book. You may be wondering, *does she ever just let it go?* I implore you right now, "Don't judge me." We don't have the ability to tell pain when it will strike or resurface in our lives. This devastation didn't only affect me. I had a son who was left to walk a path of shame, because of "us." My youngest was still school age at the time of our marital trouble. I wanted to show him a strong mother, one who could bounce back from anything. I wanted him to know God's strength, love, and provision, but the battle was overwhelming. *Bitterness becomes a destructive force, when left to fester.* I blamed God, I blamed my ex, and yes, I blamed her. Most of all I think I blamed myself. On top of it, how could he have simply moved on after toying with my heart back and forth?

Once again, I was bitter because he allowed her to come in between us, and bitter because it seemed she had the upper hand. The funny thing about bitterness is, it does little to destroy those you're angry at. Bitterness would not make them pay for disrupting my life's plan. Bitterness isn't the cure for hurt. It is a false antidote that doesn't even numb the pain.

I tried to let it all go. There were moments where I'd feel fine, and the next moment, I'd be back in that place of brokenness. I could feel God pressing me to move forward. When I laid down at night, I would hear God saying, "Give it to me, I can fix it." I cried hard into my pillow as I reminded Him of my pain and how I tried to do right as a Christian. Can you imagine me attempting to plead my case to God, like I was a defense attorney? Defense. The mechanism, that produces self-protection, it carefully guards the ego, it rests in denial, and breathes through blame. Surely, I didn't deserve this much pain.

I sounded just like Job. I mentioned him in Chapter 4. If you aren't familiar with his story, let me give a brief background. The Bible says Job was an upright man, but the Lord gave Satan, the devil, permission to attack Job's life. Job's children died, he lost his money, and then he got sick. Job reminded God of all the good things he had done and questioned why he was undergoing such extreme trial. Sound familiar? Even though Job was a good man, he wasn't perfect, and neither am I. The amazing thing is, it took me finally getting quiet enough about the pain to hear God in the first place. His healing was available seven years ago, only I was in too much misery to receive it. Now, after gaining clarity, I could hear Him, but was too afraid to take down the walls I had built. God kept speaking to me and I kept responding with the same answers. I wrestled with God for a couple of weeks, but despite my resistance, He never stopped pursuing me.

There's an old saying, "Your arms are too short to box with God." I found it to be true. I decided I was going to finally surrender. But it would not be an easy task. I needed God to submit to my stipulations. Yes, I honestly thought my rules would apply, but that isn't how God works. I got on the floor in my closet and began to weep. I could hear His soft still voice saying, "Give it to me. I promise, it will be okay." It was like my heart was in my hands and I was holding on so tight. I stretched out my hands to put it in God's hands and I broke down. I kept saying, "God, I can't. You ... let him hurt me."

I continued trying to fight for several minutes. I put it in God's hands, but I wouldn't let go. I could literally see us doing a tug of war back and forth. He kept saying, "Let it go daughter, I want to heal you."

I screamed, "I'm afraid." Finally, I said, "God, okay, I'm going to give it to you today." I could see myself placing it in His hands and there was a release. I broke down and began to wail. As I cried, I told God although I was willing to release it that day, I couldn't promise that there would not be days when I'd want to take it back. Days where I'd want the control. And truthfully, there were those days. I didn't want to be hurt anymore by anyone. But God kept assuring me of His love for me and He promised He would always be there for me.

That was the start of my healing. I cried for days after that, sometimes hours at a time, to the point that my face would be swollen. God was breaking the hardness off my heart. I spent time in prayer on the floor. I asked Him to take out all the ugliness that made my heart dark, cold, callous, unforgiving, hateful, and fearful. I wanted to be free, which also meant, dealing with my unrepentant sin. This beautiful Scripture in Isaiah 30:18 tells us that the Lord waits to be gracious to us. 1 Peter 3:20 tells us that even in our disobedience, the patience of God waits! His mercy and love are like no other. Remember Jesus waited four days to come to Lazarus. His waiting was a divine set up for a greater plan.

NUGGET:

Love waited on me, just as
He graciously waits on you.

CHAPTER SEVEN:

LOVE MADE ME WAIT

The journey toward wholeness is ongoing. On this path to self-discovery, I'm learning to embrace the "me" God has predestined. I was still learning this back then, but often, God will make us wait before answering a call for help. It's like a parent who runs to a baby every time the baby cries. There are times when you must let the child cry. If not, you will have a spoiled son or daughter. He was teaching me patience and building my faith. He has also taught me that He restores the broken. While it seems too hard to fathom, I do not regret the moments of distrust. I realize my story is one of grace. I pray that it enables others to walk in the freedom that I strove so desperately to find.

Unfortunately, I was too consumed with the big picture or how everyone else would perceive us as a divorced couple. The obsession with the opinions of others will only lead to the need for greater validation. While we are seeking the acceptance of others, our hearts can never fully embrace the love and acceptance of God. Consequently, I could only see a hazed future under disappointment and failure. And unknown to me at the time, God is always working out the details.

Romans 8:28 has become the core Scripture for my life. "And we know that all things work together for good to them that love God, to them who are the called according to his purpose."

Once my heart became pliable again, God was able to reveal Himself to me in many ways. I'd finally come to know Him as Lord. It took that brokenness to set me on a path that would change my entire life. Proverbs 4:23 says, "Guard your heart above all else, for it determines the course of your life." (NLT) The hurt, pain, loss, and shame birthed the woman I am today.

When I look back at the days of disappointment and the years of yearning to know why it took so much for me to get here, a Scripture from Isaiah reverberates loud in my spirit. Isaiah 61:3 says, "I will give you beauty for ashes." Ashes represent the residue of anything that has been destroyed. God knows that any type of pain will leave fragments or remains. He offers us beauty in exchange for the ashes. His promise motivates us to release the torn pieces so that He can restore them. No matter how broken you are, God can make all things new. I look back and I see the beauty in what He was trying to achieve in my life. It was necessary.

God wanted to give me a part of Himself. I honestly have no words for His love for me. Only God can love me like that. He used my marital situation to break me, shatter my life like a broken mirror, and leave me seemingly unrepairable. But He didn't leave me in that state. He took His time and put me back together piece by piece. He didn't just restore me, He had to reveal the areas of decay in the crevices of my heart. Along with being closed, it also held on to bondage. I saw how I could easily justify my actions and flaws while pointing out my ex-husbands. God revealed how deeply rejection caused me to accept an affair, as long as "she knew her place." She didn't have a place. When I was tired of praying, I left my marriage unguarded. This was after he'd asked to come back home but was still seeing her. Not wanting him to leave me again, I allowed her into our life. I was still thinking that I was in control. "As long as she knew her place," I said this craziness like I held the cards. Love had become so tainted and distorted that somehow I thought, *lower expectations would lessen the pain.* I was wrong!

Rejection has a way of masking itself so that we hardly recognize it when it rears its ugly head. God begin to deal with me about my past. I thought I needed to be healed from my marriage and divorce, but the pain went much deeper. Once He revealed the roots of rejection, we could deal with "acceptance." Acceptance is deeper than it appears. It centers itself in confidence. God being the master craftsman, knowing how delicate I am, was able to pull back each layer, and renew me in every area.

Being confident that God loves and accepts us, eradicates the falsehood that fake validation creates. I lost my identity in my marriage. Regardless of how beautiful it began, the stench of insecurity on both ends created chaos in different ways. Where he sought a distraction for his own pain, I sought validation for mine. I thought my love for him was enough; truthfully, a man who doesn't love himself, cannot pour from an empty source. Only God could fill the place I longed to touch. As I realized that for him, I also realized my addiction to love came from the scars of previous relationships. God didn't want me to continue down the same destructive path. Rejection could no longer flourish in my life. Through a series of processes, God was molding me.

After an unfaithful spouse, many women become bitter and resentful towards other women. They find it difficult to trust and befriend them. However, God was preparing me for the ministry to the wounded. He especially gave me a heart for women. He filled me with compassion. It speaks volumes when a woman devalues herself to date, fling, or sleep with married men, or a series of men. God allowed me into those painful places, so I could feel deep enough to help women without judgment and criticism. My heart began to open; the thing that hurt me to my core, became a channel for my healing.

I completely surrendered to the process. It wasn't cut and dry. Nothing of value is. I was becoming better and learning that true love is accompanied by forgiveness. I said, "I forgave them" a million times. But the pain of the affair crippled me and seemed to paralyze my entire life. I couldn't seem to move forward. I thought I had forgiven them. It's always been my heart to see the best in everyone. I didn't realize it was bitterness and resentment that barricaded my heart. Overcoming bitterness means intentionally releasing the hurt to God. Seek therapy if necessary.

The hard part was forgetting. I mentioned earlier how the enemy will toy with our minds. It was a true battlefield for me. The Bible warns us to cast down vain imaginations and to think on things that are pure and of good report. Being an analytical person, I try to make sense of things. I try to rationalize it. I need to know the reason behind everything. For me, things must make sense. But God was calling me to abandon myself and allow Him to take full control.

God loved me so much that He was willing to wait. I had it all wrong. I thought I was waiting on Him, but because He loved me, He was waiting for me. That is where the title of this book comes from. His love made me wait! I waited for my answers, for my healing, and for my deliverance. In the waiting, I was being developed.

The love of God is simply amazing.

Though I thought I should have written this book years ago, I now know the process from death to life was not yet complete. He was still working on me. And the process is ongoing.

When I look back, He has been glorified. People have watched my life, some up close and others from afar. They watched me being torn down but they also saw God completely restore everything in my life.

I didn't know it then, but this was never so much about my divorce, my ex-husband, or the other women. Their journey is their own. This was about me and God. He wanted to be glorified through my life, but it took my surrender and obedience. It was a tough season and I still cry at times, but they are more tears of victory over death because I chose life. I look back and see where He brought me from and where I am today and there is joy and peace that cannot be disturbed.

Not only has God taught me about His love for me. He taught me about the way I should love others. My consistent prayer is, "God give me a heart like Yours." A popular consensus is that God is one way, and we, although in His image, can totally reflect something opposite. That's not possible.

If I am a Christian, then I am or should be imitating Christ which means I should imitate His love. Loving people who hurt or wound is a deliberate choice. I can't lie, at times, it is a struggle. However, God reminds me of what I've done to Him, and it brings a humbling experience. He doesn't do it to put me down. He reminds me so that I am forever grateful for His grace towards me. I find that healing comes with each release.

The enemy will cause you to replay the hurtful words and actions in your mind. Release to God as often as you need too. Jesus Christ tells us that His yoke is light. We can never over burden God. He wants us to be open and honest about our feelings. There is beauty for ashes!

Life hasn't always been the way I intended but I can honestly say it is because of the hard times in my life I've learned to appreciate the good times. During the stormy weather, I came to know Him as God and to experience the warmth and security of His love.

Throughout my life, He has remained consistent and He has always been here. He brought me joy in sorrow and through death gave me new life. I no longer ponder with uncertainty as to the meaning of situations that occur in my life. I now know He is the Lord of my life, past, present, and future.

This is my story of pure love. The Love that loved me, also hurt me. The Love that didn't give me what I wanted, gave me what I needed. It is the story of wise love. The Love that saw me; sees me, and still loves me despite my frailties.

John 11:43-44 states, "And when he thus had spoken, he cried with a loud voice, Lazarus, come forth. And he that was dead came forth, bound hand and foot with graveclothes: and his face was bound about with a napkin. Jesus saith unto them, Loose him, and let him go."

The verses above reveal a new beginning. We are privy to the lives of Mary, Martha, and Lazarus. We witness the pain, turmoil, and trials before the miracle. However, that isn't always the case. When we become of age, we often meet people in their glory (beauty) season. We see them successful, victorious, walking with the Lord, and if not completely whole, we meet them progressing toward wholeness. Their picture of triumph and victory is so glorious (as the saying goes, "I don't look like what I've been through") that we can fail to realize that there were tests, trials, and tribulations. Ecclesiastes 3:11, says God makes all things beautiful in time. Allowing God to take the messy parts of my life and give me joy, peace, and serenity, set me on the path of self-discovery and greater purpose.

Just as Lazarus was finally loosed from everything that held him bound, God is able to loose the bondage (ashes) in your life. The wonderful thing about God, is when He removes the pain and replaces it with His healing, we are no longer numb to it; we are free to embrace what was, while looking ahead into the future. The Bible tells us that while a woman is in labor, she is in excruciating pain, but after she births the baby, she remembers the pain no more. That is the place God's love takes us. The painful past is a memory we should use to reveal God's glory. It is the testimony of a life encapsulated (surrounded) in grace. A grace that taught me that real love can never be counterfeit, because it emanates from an inexhaustible source. That Source is God.

Many pieces of my life were scattered like leaves in the wind. At times, I thought I gathered myself enough to move on and without warning, like a gust of wind that re-scatters freshly raked leaves, my life would be a mess all over again. In time, I learned the true essence of sustaining grace. Sustainment happens when we release what we think we need to hold. God's grace covers our sins, and it's all-sufficient power enables us to emerge victorious in trying circumstances. What the enemy plotted for my demise, ended in my emergence. I could have gotten a horrible sexually transmitted disease. I could have ripped them both to shreds and been jailed. I could have ended up in an insane asylum, but God's grace shielded and protected me. That same grace is available to you.

We each have our own destiny and journey. For those of you like me, the death of things in your life, will produce new life for future generations. When Lazarus was resurrected, he still needed to be loosed from the bandages. Scripture says he was bound by grave clothes, and his face bound by a napkin. Jesus commanded them to loose him, and let him go. Don't negate the process of being loosed. Restoration may be in process, but each layer of bondage still must be removed. As this book ends, I'm reminded of the time I thought lower expectations, meant I'd be prepared for the pain. And many women feel the same. I can't count how many women utter phrases like, "All men cheat." Or "He's just a man." Manhood isn't a license to be unfaithful in any area. Nor does it mean that we should accept unfaithfulness as "normal." If unfaithfulness shows up, know there must be a root. The Bible tells us if one is unfaithful in little, he will be unfaithful in much. (Luke 16:10)

A little leeway ends up being a much larger gateway. With unfaithfulness comes deceit, dishonesty, trickery, bribery, even death and murder to name a few. These will become generational sins until someone stands up and declares the chain be broken.

There is nothing like a boy trapped inside of a man's body who is forced to make adult decisions and commitments without the redemption of Christ. Loyalty is a deliberate choice. By the same token, it takes just as much intentionality for a woman to examine the relationship, she has with herself. Out of that relationship she can build a foundation to receive the purest love. Self-love has become a prominent theme in today's culture. For self-love to permeate the soul, the objective must be wholeness. Those of you reading this book have your own story. God wants to use some of you as a type of Lazarus. Because of your sacrifice, someone else will come to Christ and know the glorious power of resurrection.

I shared the worst part of my life, so that you know you are not alone. The truth is it's more difficult because we don't yield to the process. We rebel against what God is doing in our lives. Thus, the process is longer. We encounter detours. The blessing is those detours don't obliterate (cancel out) our destiny. God restores the lost and wasted time.

Some people will never pick up a Bible, but they will watch your life. We all are required to live one that exemplifies Christ. That life should include everything in Galatians 5:22-23. "But the fruit of the Spirit is love, joy, peace, patience, kindness, goodness, faithfulness, gentleness, self-control; against such things there is no law."

I haven't perfected all these things, but I am working on them, and He is still working on me. As you have read, the best part is realizing that even contaminated and distorted love, can be re-filtered through Christ, thereby producing the purest love. God's love is beyond mere words. I have tried to articulate it but when I try to describe Him, my words fail me. Each time, I am left with in awe.

The Bible says, "For God so loved the world, that He gave His only begotten Son" (John 3:16a). His love is because *He* gave. His love is without stipulation. His love is pure. Where His love is, there are no voids. His love is complete. 1 John 4:18 says, "There is no fear in love; but perfect love casteth out fear; because fear hath torment. He that feareth is not made perfect in love." Real love has the ability to remove fear. It makes you feel safe. God's love is perfect and complete. It empowers us to live beyond us and grow to become all that He says we can become. God's love is everything I'm not, and is also everything He says I can be. He encompasses love. It is everything about who He is, not even what He does. Just because, He is love.

Many ask the question, if God is love, then why does He allow pain? His response is always, "I did it because I love you and I did it for My glory." It took me a while, but I have finally come to realize that His love is outside of my human understanding. His ways are not our ways, nor His thoughts like our thoughts. We must simply trust that His will, is the best will for our lives.

NUGGET:

Remember, no matter where you are in life, what you have done or what you are going through,
God loves you.

ENDNOTES

Chapter 1

1. Strong's Greek: 5479. χαρά (chara) -- joy, delight (biblehub.com)
2. Strong's Greek: 5485 xáris [charis]. ("grace") (biblehub.com)
3. NAS Exhaustive Concordance of the Bible with Hebrew-Aramaic and Greek Dictionaries Copyright © 1981, 1998 by The Lockman FoundationAll rights reserved Lockman.org
4. "Dictionary by Merriam-Webster: America's Most-Trusted Online Dictionary." *Merriam-Webster*, Merriam-Webster, http://www.merriam-webster.com/love. accessed 03.23.2023

Chapter 3

1. "Dictionary by Merriam-Webster: America's Most-Trusted Online Dictionary." *Merriam-Webster*, Merriam-Webster, http://www.merriam-webster.com/sick. accessed 03.23.2023

Chapter 5

1. "Dictionary by Merriam-Webster: America's Most-Trusted
2. Online Dictionary." *Merriam-Webster*, Merriam-Webster, http://www.merriam-webster.com/stink. accessed 03.23.20
3. John 11:24 Commentaries: Martha said to Him, "I know that he will rise again in the resurrection on the last day." (biblehub.com)

About The Author

Michelle Drew was raised in the small country town of Sweeny, Texas. She is a teacher and an intercessor with a special passion for ministering and mentoring young women. She is a dedicated leader with a servant's heart, a woman of strength, integrity, and grace. Michelle is a woman who has faced adversity because of her own personal failures but has learned to triumph with an unwavering spirit.

In humility, Michelle encourages people by reminding them that there is nothing special about her. She is an ordinary woman committed to inspiring greatness in the lives of others. Her much anticipated book, *Love Made Me Wait*, outlines and displays publicly the private areas of her past pain.

In *Love Made Me Wait*, you will walk through the season of struggles that made her a firm believer of Romans 8:28. "And we know that all things work together for good, to them that love God, to them who are the called according to his purpose."

www.ingramcontent.com/pod-product-compliance
Lightning Source LLC
Chambersburg PA
CBHW071227160426
43196CB00012B/2442